ECONOMIC

CALCULATION

IN THE

SOCIALIST

COMMONWEALTH

Ludwig von Mises

(translated from the German by S. Adler)

The Ludwig von Mises Institute
Auburn, Alabama 36849-5301

Published by Praxeology Press of the Ludwig von Mises Institute, Auburn University, Auburn, Alabama 36849.

Library of Congress Catalog Card Number: 90-061585

ISBN: 0-945466-07-2

Contents

Foreword

The twentieth century has witnessed the beginning, development, and end of the most tragic experiment in human history: socialism. The experiment resulted in tremendous human losses, destruction of potentially rich economies, and colossal ecological disasters. The experiment has ended, but the devastation will affect the lives and health of generations to come.

The real tragedy of this experiment is that Ludwig von Mises and his followers—among the best economic minds of this century—had exposed the truth about socialism in 1920, yet their warnings went unheeded.

In this essay, "Economic Calculation in the Socialist Commonwealth," Mises examines Marxism's most fundamental claims. In doing so, Mises exposes socialism as a utopian scheme that is illogical, uneconomic, and unworkable at its core. It is "impossible" and must fail because it is devoid of economic rationale; it provides no means for any objective basis of economic calculation and thus no way to assign resources to their most productive uses. In 1920, however, the enthusiasm for socialism was so strong, especially among Western intellectuals, that Mises's short and insightful masterpiece was either not understood or deliberately distorted by his critics.

Yet the actual implementation of socialism showed the complete validity of his analysis. Socialism attempted to replace billions of individual decisions made by sovereign consumers in the market with "rational economic planning" by a few vested with the power to determine the who, what, how, and when of production and consumption. It led to widespread shortages, starvation, and mass frustration of the population. When the Soviet government set 22 million prices, 460,000 wage rates, and over 90 million work quotas for 110 million government employees, chaos and shortages were the inevitable result. The socialist state destroyed work ethic, deprived people of entrepreneurial opportunity and initiative, and led to a widespread welfare mentality.

Socialism produced political monsters like Stalin and Mao Tse-Tung, and led to unheard-of crimes against humanity in all communist states. The destruction of Russia and Kampuchea, the humiliation of the Chinese and Eastern European people, are not "distortions of socialism" as the defenders of this doctrine would like to convince us: they are inevitable consequences of the destruction of the market which started with an attempt to replace the economic decisions of free individuals by the "wisdom of the planners."

The real character of the so-called centrally planned economy is well illustrated by a quip I heard several years ago by Soviet economist Nikolai Fedorenko. He said that a fully balanced, checked, and detailed economic plan for the next year would be ready, with the help of computers, in 30,000 years. There are millions of product variants; there are hundreds of thousands of enterprises; it is necessary to make billions of decisions on inputs and outputs; the plans must relate to labor force, material supplies, wages, costs, prices, "planned profits," investments, transportation, storage, and distribution. These decisions originate from different parts of the planning hierarchy. They are, as a rule, inconsistent and contradictory to each other because they reflect the conflicting interests of different strata of bureaucracy. Because the next year's plan must be ready by next year, and not in 29,999 years, it is inevitably neither balanced nor rational. And Mises proved that without private property in the means of production, even with 30,000 years of computer time, they still couldn't make socialism work.

The defenders of socialism found themselves in a theoretical and practical deadlock as soon as they destroyed the institution of private property. Thus they resorted to the creation of artificial schemes. In the Soviet economy, profit is planned as a function of the cost. Enterprises are given "control figures" which determine the "planned profits" as a percentage of the costs. Thus the more you spend, the higher your profits. Under conditions of 100% monopolization, this simple device completely ruined the economies of the Soviet Union, Eastern Europe, and other "socialist" states to an extent comparable only to the barbarian invasions of Rome.

Today, the disastrous consequences of enforcing the utopia on the unfortunate populations of the communist states are clear even to their leaders. As Mises predicted, despite the "cloud-cuckoo lands of their fancy," roasted pigeons failed to fly into the mouths of the comrades. And even according to official Soviet statistics, 234 of 277 basic consumer goods included by the USSR State Committee on Statistics in the "market basket" of the Soviet people are "missing" from the state distribution system.

Yet Western advocates of socialism are still singing the old tune about the necessity to restrict property rights and replace the market with the "wisdom" of rational central planning.

In 1920, the world neglected or rejected Mises's warning that "socialism is the abolition of rational economy." We cannot afford to repeat this mistake today. We must stay alert to all schemes that would draw us into a new round of state experimentation on the people and the economy.

"Private property of the material factors of production," Mises emphasized, "is not a restriction of the freedom of all other people to choose what suits them. It is, on the contrary, the means that assigns to the common man in his capacity as a buyer, supremacy in all economic affairs. It is the means to stimulate a nation's most enterprising men to exert themselves to the best of their abilities in the service of all of the people."

We must never again forget or ignore the insights of this great thinker, for the sake of liberty and the generations to come.

Yuri N. Maltsev
Senior Fellow, International Center for Development Policy; The Ludwig von Mises Institute; and Senior Researcher, Institute of Economics, Academy of Sciences, USSR (1987-89)
April 1990

Introduction
to this Edition

Ludwig von Mises's seminal refutation of socialist economics, republished here, was written seventy years ago, but it is a description of the "real socialism" of today—or rather yesterday. Mises's thesis is that in a socialist economy rational economic calculation is impossible; its attempts to allocate resources efficiently in the absence of private ownership of the means of production must fail. The East Bloc's disastrous experience with socialism has shown the world that Mises was correct all along.

In this article, Mises writes of full-blown socialism, where the state is the sole owner of the means of production. Although made so long ago, his description reflects very well the economic realities of the Soviet Union since the late twenties, and of Central and Eastern Europe since the late forties until, practically, today.

In the socialist economy that Mises described, consumption goods are freely demanded and exchanged by individuals of different tastes. Money can exist, but only within the limited sphere of the market for consumer goods. In the sphere of production, however, there is no private ownership of the means of production. They are not exchanged, and as a consequence, it is impossible to establish prices that reflect actual conditions. If there are no prices, there is no method of finding the most effective combination of the factors of production.

Mises's pathbreaking article led to a famous debate on socialist calculation. Polish economist Oskar Lange contested Mises's position and tried to show that socialism can work by a "trial and error" method.[1] In the Lange model, the economy has a free market for consumption goods. The production sphere is organized into enterprises and branches, and there is a Central Planning Board. The bosses of enterprises are required to establish production plans in exactly the same way the private entrepreneurs would do—in a way that minimizes costs and makes marginal cost equal to price. The Central Planning Board determines the rate of investment, the volume and structure of public goods, and the prices of all inputs. The rate of investment is established by equating the demand and supply of capital goods. The Board raises the prices when the demand is not satisfied and lowers them when supply is too large.

Presuming for a moment that this would work, the question arises: why is this method better than the real market? For Lange, there were two advantages. First, income can be more equally distributed. Since there is no capital income, people are paid according to their input labor. (Some talented people receive additional income which is a sort of "rent" on their particular skills.) Second, socialism allows for better planning of long-term

[1]Oskar Lange, "On the Economic Theory of Socialism," *Review of Economic Studies* (1936-37).

investment. Investment will not be directed by short-term fluctuation of opinions about future opportunities, and thus it would be less wasteful and more rational. Similar to John Maynard Keynes and, later, Paul Samuelson, Lange thought that although the free market may give proper signals concerning short-term production decisions, it does not give long-term signals concerning investment.

Lange used neoclassical, not Marxist terminology. Although he was a socialist by conviction, he was fascinated by the intellectual side of marginalist economics and by the possibility of showing with this apparatus that Mises was wrong. Lange thought that, theoretically, the possibility of calculation without an actual market was shown by the Italian economist Enrico Barone in 1908.[2] Barone referred to a system of general equilibrium saying that if the sets of equations could be solved, the partial equilibria of producers and consumers could be established *ex ante*. Barone's point was, however, that such a possibility is practically impossible, so (similar to Mises) he supported the view that socialism cannot work efficiently. Lange's aim was to show that both Mises and Barone were wrong (but Mises to a larger degree) and that theoretically and practically, calculation was possible.

---

[2]Enrico Barone, "Il ministerio della produzione nello stato collettivista," *Giornale degli Economisti e Revista di Statistica*, vol 37 (1908).

Lange thought he had finally solved the problems of socialist calculation that Mises had demonstrated in his essay "Economic Calculation in the Socialist Commonwealth." And to this point Lange wrote in his article "On the Economic Theory of Socialism":

> Socialists have certainly good reason to be grateful to Professor Mises, the great *advocatus diaboli* of their cause. For it was his powerful challenge that forced the socialists to recognize the importance of an adequate system of economic accounting to guide the allocation of resources in a socialist economy. Even more, it was chiefly due to Professor Mises' challenge that many socialists became aware of the very existence of such a problem.... [T]he merit of having caused the socialists to approach this problem systematically belongs entirely to Professor Mises.

Thus Lange suggested the following:

> Both as an expression of recognition for the great service rendered by him and as a memento of the prime importance of sound economic accounting, a statue of Professor Mises ought to occupy an honorable place in the great hall of the Ministry of Socialization or of the Central Planning Board of the socialist state.

Lange's theoretical views, as well as his conviction of the practical applicability of a "shadow market" in the socialist economy, were, in turn, questioned by Friedrich A. Hayek.[3] Hayek thought that Lange had committed many errors. In Lange's version

---

[3]Friedrich A. Hayek, "Socialist Calculation: the Competitive 'Solution'," *Economica*, n.s., vol. vii, no. 26 (1940).

of socialism, an army of controllers would be needed to verifythe calculations of the heads of enterprises. But what would motivate the heads of enterprises and branches? Would they be prevented from cheating. Moreover, the results of these calculations would have to be compared with additional, counter-factual calculations in order to see whether the bosses of enterprises have chosen the best combination of factors of production possible. All this would call for an enormous bureaucratic state.

The practical side of socialism took its own course. A communist economy as we know it was constructed in the Soviet Union in the late twenties and early thirties and then transplanted to Central and Eastern Europe after World War II. For a time it seemed to have worked well, at least from the point of view of the ruling bureaucracies, who did not hesitate to use totalitarian measures and mass terror.

There was no place for private ownership, nor for the market. The only method of coordinating economic activity was government command and bureaucratic allocation. The result was a prolonged crisis, marked by a stagnation or decrease of production, by inflation, ecological disaster (because of wasteful use of all types of resources—energy, water, forests, etc.), by falling standards of living, and by widespread public frustration and social pathology. This crisis, coupled with political developments including the rise of an organized opposition, brought about the revolutionary changes we witnessed in 1989.

In Eastern European countries, and in Poland in particular, there is now a strong desire to reintroduce private property and the free market.

When it has been accomplished, perhaps Lange's suggestion should be taken up: a statue of Mises should be erected in Poland—in tribute to his final intellectual triumph. For his vision of a free society provides firm intellectual grounding for the emergence of a free and prosperous Poland.

Jacek Kochanowicz
Professor of Economics
University of Warsaw, Poland
April 1990

Economic Calculation
in the Socialist Commonwealth

Ludwig von Mises

Introduction

There are many socialists who have never come to grips
in any way with the problems of economics, and who have
made no attempt at all to form for themselves any clear
conception of the conditions which determine the character of human society. There are others, who have probed
deeply into the economic history of the past and present,
and striven, on this basis, to construct a theory of economics of the "bourgeois" society. They have criticized freely
enough the economic structure of "free" society, but have
consistently neglected to apply to the economics of the
disputed socialist state the same caustic acumen, which
they have revealed elsewhere, not always with success.
Economics, as such, figures all too sparsely in the glamor-
ous pictures painted by the Utopians. They invariably

[This article appeared originally under the title "Die Wirtschaftsrechnung
im sozialistischen Gemeinwesen" in the *Archiv für Sozialwissenschaften*, vol.
47 (1920). The present translation was first published in F. A. Hayek, ed.,
Collectivist Economic Planning (London: George Routledge & Sons, 1935;
reprint, Clifton, N. J.: Augustus M. Kelley, 1975), pp. 87-130. Some annota-
tions appear in this edition and they are set aside in brackets.]

explain how, in the cloud-cuckoo lands of their fancy, roast pigeons will in some way fly into the mouths of the comrades, but they omit to show how this miracle is to take place. Where they do in fact commence to be more explicit in the domain of economics, they soon find themselves at a loss—one remembers, for instance, Proudhon's fantastic dreams of an "exchange bank"—so that it is not difficult to point out their logical fallacies. When Marxism solemnly forbids its adherents to concern themselves with economic problems beyond the expropriation of the expropriators, it adopts no new principle, since the Utopians throughout their descriptions have also neglected all economic considerations, and concentrated attention solely upon painting lurid pictures of existing conditions and glowing pictures of that golden age which is the natural consequence of the New Dispensation.

Whether one regards the coming of socialism as an unavoidable result of human evolution, or considers the socialization of the means of production as the greatest blessing or the worst disaster that can befall mankind, one must at least concede, that investigation into the conditions of society organized upon a socialist basis is of value as something more than "a good mental exercise, and a means of promoting political clearness and consistency of thought."[1] In an age in which we are approaching nearer and nearer to socialism, and even, in a certain

---

[1] Karl Kautsky, *The Social Revolution and On the Morrow of the Social Revolution* (London: Twentieth Century Press, 1907), Part II, p. 1.

sense, are dominated by it, research into the problems of the socialist state acquires added significance for the explanation of what is going on around us. Previous analyses of the exchange economy no longer suffice for a proper understanding of social phenomena in Germany and its eastern neighbors today. Our task in this connection is to embrace within a fairly wide range the elements of socialistic society. Attempts to achieve clarity on this subject need no further justification.

1.
The Distribution of Consumption Goods in the Socialist Commonwealth

Under socialism all the means of production are the property of the community. It is the community alone which can dispose of them and which determines their use in production. It goes without saying that the community will only be in a position to employ its powers of disposal through the setting up of a special body for the purpose. The structure of this body and the question of how it will articulate and represent the communal will is for us of subsidiary importance. One may assume that this last will depend upon the choice of personnel, and in cases where the power is not vested in a dictatorship, upon the majority vote of the members of the corporation.

The owner of production goods, who has manufactured consumption goods and thus becomes their owner, now has the choice of either consuming them himself or of having them consumed by others. But where the community becomes the owner of consumption goods, which it has acquired in production, such a choice will no longer obtain. It cannot itself consume; it has perforce to allow others to do so. Who is to do the consuming and what is to be consumed by each is the crux of the problem of socialist distribution.

It is characteristic of socialism that the distribution of consumption goods must be independent of the question of production and of its economic conditions. It is irreconcilable with the nature of the communal ownership of production goods that it should rely even for a part of its distribution upon the economic imputation of the yield to the particular factors of production. It is logically absurd to speak of the worker's enjoying the "full yield" of his work, and then to subject to a separate distribution the shares of the material factors of production. For, as we shall show, it lies in the very nature of socialist production that the shares of the particular factors of production in the national dividend cannot be ascertained, and that it is impossible in fact to gauge the relationship between expenditure and income.

What basis will be chosen for the distribution of consumption goods among the individual comrades is for us a consideration of more or less secondary importance. Whether they will be apportioned according to individual needs, so that he gets most who needs most, or whether the superior man is to receive more than the inferior, or whether a strictly equal distribution is envisaged as the ideal, or whether service to the State is to be the criterion, is immaterial to the fact that, in any event, the portions will be meted out by the State.

Let us assume the simple proposition that distribution will be determined upon the principle that the State treats all its members alike; it is not difficult to conceive of a number of peculiarities such as age, sex, health, occupation, etc., according to which what each receives will be graded. Each comrade receives a bundle of coupons, redeemable within a certain period against a definite quantity of certain specified goods. And so he can eat several times a day, find permanent lodgings, occasional amusements and a new suit every now and again. Whether such provision for these needs is ample or not, will depend on the productivity of social labor.

Moreover, it is not necessary that every man should consume the whole of his portion. He may let some of it perish without consuming it; he may give it away in presents; he many even in so far as the nature of the goods permit, hoard it for future use. He can, however, also exchange some of them. The beer tippler will gladly dispose of non-alcoholic drinks allotted to him, if he can get more beer in exchange, whilst the teetotaler will be ready to give up his portion of drink if he can get other goods for it. The art lover will be willing to dispose of his cinema tickets in order the more often to hear good music; the Philistine will be quite prepared to give up the tickets which admit him to art exhibitions in return for opportunities for pleasure he more readily understands. They will all welcome exchanges. But the material of these exchanges will always be consumption goods. Production goods in a socialist commonwealth are exclusively communal; they are an inalienable property of the community, and thus *res extra commercium*.

The principle of exchange can thus operate freely in a socialist state within the narrow limits permitted. It need not always develop in the form of direct exchanges. The same grounds which have always existed for the building-up of indirect exchange will continue in a socialist state, to place advantages in the way of those who indulge in it. It follows that the socialist state will thus also afford room for the use of a universal medium of exchange—that is, of money. Its role will be fundamentally the same in a socialist as in a competitive society; in both it serves as the universal medium of exchange. Yet the significance of money in a society where the means of production are State controlled will be different from that which attaches to it in one where they are privately owned. It will be, in fact, incomparably narrower, since the material available for exchange will be narrower, inasmuch as it will be confined to consumption goods. Moreover, just because no production good will ever become the object of exchange, it will be impossible to determine its monetary value. Money could never fill in a socialist state the role it fills in a competitive society in determining the value of production goods. Calculation in terms of money will here be impossible.

The relationships which result from this system of

exchange between comrades cannot be disregarded by those responsible for the administration and distribution of products. They must take these relationships as their basis, when they seek to distribute goods per head in accordance with their exchange value. If, for instance 1 cigar becomes equal to 5 cigarettes, it will be impossible for the administration to fix the arbitrary value of 1 cigar = 3 cigarettes as a basis for the equal distribution of cigars and cigarettes respectively. If the tobacco coupons are not to be redeemed uniformly for each individual, partly against cigars, partly against cigarettes, and if some receive only cigars and others only cigarettes, either because that is their wish or because the coupon office cannot do anything else at the moment, the market conditions of exchange would then have to be observed. Otherwise everybody getting cigarettes would suffer as against those getting cigars. For the man who gets one cigar can exchange it for five cigarettes, and he is only marked down with three cigarettes.

Variations in exchange relations in the dealings between comrades will therefore entail corresponding variations in the administrations' estimates of the representative character of the different consumption-goods. Every such variation shows that a gap has appeared between the particular needs of comrades and their satisfactions because in fact, some one commodity is more strongly desired than another.

The administration will indeed take pains to bear this point in mind also as regards production. Articles in greater demand will have to be produced in greater quantities while production of those which are less demanded will have to suffer a curtailment. Such control may be possible, but one thing it will not be free to do; it must not leave it to the individual comrade to ask the value of his tobacco ticket either in cigars or cigarettes at will. If the comrade were to have the right of choice, then it might well be that the demand for cigars and cigarettes would exceed the supply, or vice versa, that cigars or cigarettes pile up in the distributing offices because no one will take them.

If one adopts the standpoint of the labor theory of value, the problem freely admits of a simple solution. The comrade is then marked up for every hour's work put in, and this entitles him to receive the product of one hour's labor, less the amount deducted for meeting such obligations of the community as a whole as maintenance of the unfit, education, etc.

Taking the amount deducted for covering communal expenses as one half of the labor product, each worker who had worked a full hour would be entitled only to obtain such amount of the product as really answered to half an hour's work. Accordingly, anybody who is in a position to offer twice the labor time taken in manufacturing an article, could take it from the market and transfer to his own use or consumption. For the clarification of our problem it will be better to assume that the State does not in fact deduct anything from the workers towards meeting its obligations, but instead imposes an income tax on its working members. In that way every hour of work put in would carry with it the right of taking for oneself such amount of goods as entailed an hour's work.

Yet such a manner of regulating distribution would be unworkable, since labor is not a uniform and homogeneous quantity. Between various types of labor there is necessarily a qualitative difference, which leads to a different valuation according to the difference in the conditions of demand for and supply of their products. For instance, the supply of pictures cannot be increased *ceteris paribus*, without damage to the quality of the product. Yet one cannot allow the laborer who had put in an hour of the most simple type of labor to be entitled to the product of an hour's higher type of labor. Hence, it becomes utterly impossible in any socialist community to posit a connection between the significance to the community of any type of labor and the apportionment of the yield of the communal process of production. The remuneration of labor cannot but proceed upon an arbitrary basis; it cannot be based upon the economic valuation of the yield as in a competitive state of society, where the means of production are in private hands, since—as we have seen—any such valuation is impossible in a socialist community. Economic realities impose clear limits to the community's power of fixing the remuneration of labor on an arbitrary basis: in no circumstances can the sum expended on wages exceed the income for any length of time.

Within these limits it can do as it will. It can rule forthwith that all labor is to be reckoned of equal worth, so that every hour of work, whatever its quality, entails the same reward; it can equally well make a distinction in regard to the quality of work done. Yet in both cases it must reserve the power to control the particular distribution of the labor product. It will never be able to arrange that he who has put in an hour's labor shall also have the right to consume the product of an hour's labor, even leaving aside the question of differences in the quality of the labor and the products, and assuming moreover that it would be possible to gauge the amount of labor represented by any given article. For, over and above the actual labor, the production of all economic goods entails also the cost of materials. An article in which more raw material is used can never be reckoned of equal value with one in which less is used.

2.
The Nature of Economic Calculation

Every man who, in the course of economic life, takes a choice between the satisfaction of one need as against another, *eo ipso* makes a judgment of value. Such judgments of value at once include only the very satisfaction of the need itself; and from this they reflect back upon the goods of a lower, and then further upon goods of a higher order.[2] As a rule, the man who knows his own mind is in a position to value goods of a lower order. Under simple conditions it

---

[2][By "lower order" Mises refers to those goods made for final consumption, and by "higher order" those used in production.]

is also possible for him without much ado to form some judgment of the significance to him of goods of a higher order. But where the state of affairs is more involved and their interconnections not so easily discernible, subtler means must be employed to accomplish a correct[3] valuation of the means of production. It would not be difficult for a farmer in economic isolation to come by a distinction between the expansion of pasture-farming and the development of activity in the hunting field. In such a case the processes of production involved are relatively short and the expense and income entailed can be easily gauged. But it is quite a different matter when the choice lies between the utilization of a water-course for the manufacture of electricity or the extension of a coal mine or the drawing up of plans for the better employment of the energies latent in raw coal. Here the roundabout processes of production are many and each is very lengthy; here the conditions necessary for the success of the enterprises which are to be initiated are diverse, so that one cannot apply merely vague valuations, but requires rather more exact estimates and some judgment of the economic issues actually involved.

Valuation can only take place in terms of units, yet it is impossible that there should ever be a unit of subjective use value for goods. Marginal utility does not posit any unit of value, since it is obvious that the value of two units of a given stock is necessarily greater than, but less than double, the value of a single unit. Judgments

[3]Using that term, of course, in the sense only of the valuating subject, and not in an objective and universally applicable sense.

of value do not measure; they merely establish grades and scales.[4] Even Robinson Crusoe, when he has to make a decision where no ready judgment of value appears and where he has to construct one upon the basis of a more or less exact estimate, cannot operate solely with subjective use value, but must take into consideration the inter-substitutability of goods on the basis of which he can then form his estimates. In such circumstances it will be impossible for him to refer all things back to one unit. Rather will he, so far as he can, refer all the elements which have to be taken into account in forming his estimate to those economic goods which can be apprehended by an obvious judgment of value—that is to say, to goods of a lower order and to pain-cost. That this is only possible in very simple conditions is obvious. In the case of more complicated and more lengthy processes of production it will, plainly, not answer.

In an exchange economy the objective exchange value of commodities enters as the unit of economic calculation. This entails a threefold advantage. In the first place, it renders it possible to base the calculation upon the valuations of all participants in trade. The subjective use value of each is not immediately comparable as a purely individual phenomenon with the subjective use value of other men. It only becomes so in exchange value, which arises out of the interplay of the subjective valuations of all who take part in exchange. But in that case calculation by exchange value furnishes a control over the appropriate employment of

[4]Franz Čuhel, *Zur Lehre von den Bedürfnissen* (Innsbruck: Wagner'sche Universität-Buchhandlung, 1907), pp. 198 ff.

goods. Anyone who wishes to make calculations in regard to a complicated process of production will immediately notice whether he has worked more economically than others or not; if he finds, from reference to the exchange relations obtaining in the market, that he will not be able to produce profitably, this shows that others understand how to make a better use of the goods of higher order in question. Lastly, calculation by exchange value makes it possible to refer values back to a unit. For this purpose, since goods are mutually substitutable in accordance with the exchange relations obtaining in the market, any possible good can be chosen. In a monetary economy it is money that is so chosen.

Monetary calculation has its limits. Money is no yardstick of value, nor yet of price. Value is not indeed measured in money, nor is price. They merely consist in money. Money as an economic good is not of stable value as has been naïvely, but wrongly, assumed in using it as a "standard of deferred payments." The exchange-relationship which obtains between money and goods is subjected to constant, if (as a rule) not too violent, fluctuations originating not only from the side of other economic goods, but also from the side of money. However, these fluctuations disturb value calculations only in the slightest degree, since usually, in view of the ceaseless alternations in other economic data—these calculations will refer only to comparatively short periods of time—periods in which "good" money, at least normally, undergoes comparatively trivial fluctuations in regard to its exchange relations. The inadequacy of the monetary calculation of value does not have its main-spring in the fact that value is then calculated in terms of a universal medium of exchange, namely money, but rather in the fact that in this system it is exchange value and not subjective use value on which the calculation is based. It can never obtain as a measure for the calculation of those value determining elements which stand outside the domain of exchange transactions. If, for example, a man were to calculate the profitability of erecting a waterworks, he would not be able to include in his calculation the beauty of the waterfall which the scheme might impair, except that he may pay attention to the diminution of tourist traffic or similar changes, which may be valued in terms of money. Yet these considerations might well prove one of the factors in deciding whether or not the building is to go up at all.

It is customary to term such elements "extra-economic." This perhaps is appropriate; we are not concerned with disputes over terminology; yet the considerations themselves can scarcely be termed irrational. In any place where men regard as significant the beauty of a neighborhood or of a building, the health, happiness and contentment of mankind, the honor of individuals or nations, they are just as much motive forces of rational conduct as are economic factors in the proper sense of the word, even where they are not substitutable against each other on the market and therefore do not enter into exchange relationships.

That monetary calculation cannot embrace these factors lies in its very nature; but for the purposes of our everyday economic life this does not detract from the significance of monetary calculation. For all those ideal goods are goods of a lower order, and can hence be embraced straightway within the ambit of our judgment of values. There is therefore no difficulty in taking them into account, even though they must remain outside the sphere of monetary value. That they do not admit of such computation renders their consideration in the affairs of life easier and not harder. Once we see clearly how highly we value beauty, health, honor and pride, surely nothing can prevent us from paying a corresponding regard to them. It may seem painful to any sensitive spirit to have to balance spiritual goods against material. But that is not the fault of monetary calculation; it lies in the very nature of things themselves. Even where judgments of value can be established directly without computation in value or in money, the necessity of choosing between material and spiritual satisfaction cannot be evaded. Robinson Crusoe and the socialist state have an equal obligation to make the choice.

Anyone with a genuine sense of moral values experiences no hardship in deciding between honor and livelihood. He knows his plain duty. If a man cannot make honor his bread, yet can he renounce his bread for honor's sake. Only they who prefer to be relieved of the agony of this decision, because they cannot bring themselves to renounce material comfort for the sake of spiritual advantage, see in the choice a profanation of true values.

Monetary calculation only has meaning within the sphere of economic organization. It is a system whereby the rules of economics may be applied in the disposition of economic goods. Economic goods only have part in this system in proportion to the extent to which they may be exchanged for money. Any extension of the sphere of monetary calculation causes misunderstanding. It cannot be regarded as constituting a kind of yardstick for the valuation of goods, and cannot be so treated in historical investigations into the development of social relationships; it cannot be used as a criterion of national wealth and income, nor as a means of gauging the value of goods which stand outside the sphere of exchange, as who should seek to estimate the extent of human losses through emigrations or wars in terms of money?[5] This is mere sciolistic tomfoolery, however much it may be indulged in by otherwise perspicacious economists.

Nevertheless within these limits, which in economic life it never oversteps, monetary calculation fulfils all the requirements of economic calculation. It affords us a guide through the oppressive plenitude of economic potentialities. It enables us to extend to all goods of a higher order the judgment of value, which is bound up with and clearly evident in, the case of goods ready for consumption, or at best of production goods of the lowest order. It renders their value capable of computation and thereby gives us the primary basis for all economic operations with goods of a higher order. Without it, all production involving processes stretching well back in time and all the longer

---

[5]Cf. Friedrich von Wieser, *Über den Ursprung und die Hauptgesetze des wirtschaftlichen Wertes* (Vienna: A. Hölder, 1884), pp. 185 ff.

roundabout processes of capitalistic production would be gropings in the dark.

There are two conditions governing the possibility of calculating value in terms of money. Firstly, not only must goods of a lower, but also those of a higher order, come within the ambit of exchange, if they are to be included. If they do not do so, exchange relationships would not arise. True enough, the considerations which must obtain in the case of Robinson Crusoe prepared, within the range of his own hearth, to exchange, by production, labor and flour for bread, are indistinguishable from those which obtain when he is prepared to exchange bread for clothes in the open market, and, therefore, it is to some extent true to say that every economic action, including Robinson Crusoe's own production, can be termed *exchange*.[6] Moreover, the mind of one man alone—be it ever so cunning, is too weak to grasp the importance of any single one among the countlessly many goods of a higher order. No single man can ever master all the possibilities of production, innumerable as they are, as to be in a position to make straightway evident judgments of value without the aid of some system of computation. The distribution among a number of individuals of administrative control over economic goods in a community of men who take part in the labor of producing them, and who are economically interested in them,

---

[6]Cf. Mises, *Theorie des Geldes und der Umlaufsmittel* (Munich and Leipzig: Duncker & Humblot, 1912), p. 16, with the references there given. [See the English translation by H. E. Batson, *The Theory of Money and Credit* (Indianapolis: Liberty Classics, 1980), p. 52.]

entails a kind of intellectual division of labor, which would not be possible without some system of calculating production and without economy.

The second condition is that there exists in fact a universally employed medium of exchange—namely, money—which plays the same part as a medium in the exchange of production goods also. If this were not the case, it would not be possible to reduce all exchange-relationships to a common denominator.

Only under simple conditions can economics dispense with monetary calculation. Within the narrow confines of household economy, for instance, where the father can supervise the entire economic management, it is possible to determine the significance of changes in the processes of production, without such aids to the mind, and yet with more or less of accuracy. In such a case the process develops under a relatively limited use of capital. Few of the capitalistic roundabout processes of production are here introduced: what is manufactured is, as a rule, consumption goods or at least such goods of a higher order as stand very near to consumption-goods. The division of labor is in its rudimentary stages: one and the same laborer controls the labor of what is in effect, a complete process of production of goods ready for consumption, from beginning to end. All this is different, however, in developed communal production. The experiences of a remote and bygone period of simple production do not provide any sort of argument for establishing the possibility of an economic system without monetary calculation.

In the narrow confines of a closed household economy, it is possible throughout to review the process of production from beginning to end, and to judge all the time whether one or another mode of procedure yields more consumable goods. This, however, is no longer possible in the incomparably more involved circumstances of our own social economy. It will be evident, even in the socialist society, that 1,000 hectolitres of wine are better than 800, and it is not difficult to decide whether it desires 1,000 hectolitres of wine rather than 500 of oil. There is no need for any system of calculation to establish this fact: the deciding element is the will of the economic subjects involved. But once this decision has been taken, the real task of rational economic direction only commences, i.e. economically, to place the means at the service of the end. That can only be done with some kind of economic calculation. The human mind cannot orientate itself properly among the bewildering mass of intermediate products and potentialities of production without such aid. It would simply stand perplexed before the problems of management and location.[7]

It is an illusion to imagine that in a socialist state calculation *in natura* can take the place of monetary calculation. Calculation *in natura*, in an economy without exchange, can embrace consumption goods only; it completely fails when it comes to dealing with goods of a higher

---

[7]Friedrich von Gottl-Ottlilienfeld, *Wirtschaft und Technik* (Grundriss der Sozialökonomik, Section II; Tübingen: J. C. B. Mohr, 1914), p. 216.

order. And as soon as one gives up the conception of a freely established monetary price for goods of a higher order, rational production becomes completely impossible. Every step that takes us away from private ownership of the means of production and from the use of money also takes us away from rational economics.

It is easy to overlook this fact, considering that the extent to which socialism is in evidence among us constitutes only a socialistic oasis in a society with monetary exchange, which is still a free society to a certain degree. In one sense we may agree with the socialists' assertion which is otherwise entirely untenable and advanced only as a demagogic point, to the effect that the nationalization and municipalization of enterprise is not really socialism, since these concerns in their business organizations are so much dependent upon the environing economic system with its free commerce that they cannot be said to partake today of the really essential nature of a socialist economy. In state and municipal undertakings technical improvements are introduced because their effect in similar private enterprises, domestic or foreign, can be noticed, and because those private industries which produce the materials for these improvements give the impulse for their introduction. In these concerns the advantages of reorganization can be established, because they operate within the sphere of a society based upon private ownership of the means of production and upon the system of monetary exchange, being thus capable of computation and account. This state of affairs, however, could not obtain in the case of socialist concerns operating in a purely socialistic environment.

Without economic calculation there can be no economy. Hence, in a socialist state wherein the pursuit of economic calculation is impossible, there can be—in our sense of the term—no economy whatsoever. In trivial and secondary matters rational conduct might still be possible, but in general it would be impossible to speak of rational production any more. There would be no means of determining what was rational, and hence it is obvious that production could never be directed by economic considerations. What this means is clear enough, apart from its effects on the supply of commodities. Rational conduct would be divorced from the very ground which is its proper domain. Would there, in fact, be any such thing as rational conduct at all, or, indeed, such a thing as rationality and logic in thought itself? Historically, human rationality is a development of economic life. Could it then obtain when divorced therefrom?

For a time the remembrance of the experiences gained in a competitive economy, which has obtained for some thousands of years, may provide a check to the complete collapse of the art of economy. The older methods of procedure might be retained not because of their rationality but because they appear to be hallowed by tradition. Actually, they would meanwhile have become irrational, as no longer comporting with the new conditions. Eventually, through the general reconstruction of economic thought, they will experience alterations which will render them in fact uneconomic. The supply of goods will no longer proceed anarchically of its own accord; that is true. All transactions which serve the purpose of meeting requirements will be subject to the control of a supreme authority. Yet in place of the economy of the "anarchic" method of production, recourse will be had to the senseless output of an absurd apparatus. The wheels will turn, but will run to no effect.

One may anticipate the nature of the future socialist society. There will be hundreds and thousands of factories in operation. Very few of these will be producing wares ready for use; in the majority of cases what will be manufactured will be unfinished goods and production goods. All these concerns will be interrelated. Every good will go through a whole series of stages before it is ready for use. In the ceaseless toil and moil of this process, however, the administration will be without any means of testing their bearings. It will never be able to determine whether a given good has not been kept for a superfluous length of time in the necessary processes of production, or whether work and material have not been wasted in its completion. How will it be able to decide whether this or that method of production is the more profitable? At best it will only be able to compare the quality and quantity of the consumable end product produced, but will in the rarest cases be in a position to compare the expenses entailed in production. It will know, or think it knows, the ends to be achieved by economic organization, and will have to regulate its activities accordingly, i.e. it will have to attain those ends with the least expense. It will have to make its computations with a view to finding the cheapest way. This computation will naturally have to be a value computation. It is eminently clear, and requires no further proof, that it cannot be of a technical character, and that it cannot be based upon the objective use value of goods and services.

Now, in the economic system of private ownership of the means of production, the system of computation by value is necessarily employed by each independent member of society. Everybody participates in its emergence in a double way: on the one hand as a consumer and on the other as a producer. As a consumer he establishes a scale of valuation for goods ready for use in consumption. As a producer he puts goods of a higher order into such use as produces the greatest return. In this way all goods of a higher order receive a position in the scale of valuations in accordance with the immediate state of social conditions of production and of social needs. Through the interplay of these two processes of valuation, means will be afforded for governing both consumption and production by the economic principle throughout. Every graded system of pricing proceeds from the fact that men always and ever harmonized their own requirements with their estimation of economic facts.

All this is necessarily absent from a socialist state. The administration may know exactly what goods are most urgently needed. But in so doing, it has only found what is, in fact, but one of the two necessary prerequisites for economic calculation. In the nature of the case it must, however, dispense with the other—the valuation of the means of production. It may establish the value attained by the totality of the means of production;

this is obviously identical with that of all the needs thereby satisfied. It may also be able to calculate the value of any means of production by calculating the consequence of its withdrawal in relation to the satisfaction of needs. Yet it cannot reduce this value to the uniform expression of a money price, as can a competitive economy, wherein all prices can be referred back to a common expression in terms of money. In a socialist commonwealth which, whilst it need not of necessity dispense with money altogether, yet finds it impossible to use money as an expression of the price of the factors of production (including labor), money can play no role in economic calculation.[8]

Picture the building of a new railroad. Should it be built at all, and if so, which out of a number of conceivable roads should be built? In a competitive and monetary economy, this question would be answered by monetary calculation. The new road will render less expensive the transport of some goods, and it may be possible to calculate whether this reduction of expense transcends that involved in the building and upkeep of the next line. That can only be calculated in money. It is not possible to attain the desired end merely by counterbalancing the various physical expenses and

---

[8]This fact is also recognized by Otto Neurath (*Durch die Kriegswirtschaft zur Naturalwirtschaft* [Munich: G. D. W. Callwey, 1919], pp. 216 f.). He advances the view that every complete administrative economy is, in the final analysis, a natural economy. "Socialization," he says, "is thus the pursuit of natural economy." Neurath merely overlooks the insuperable difficulties that would have to develop with economic calculation in the socialist commonwealth.

physical savings. Where one cannot express hours of labor, iron, coal, all kinds of building material, machines and other things necessary for the construction and upkeep of the railroad in a common unit it is not possible to make calculations at all. The drawing up of bills on an economic basis is only possible where all the goods concerned can be referred back to money. Admittedly, monetary calculation has its inconveniences and serious defects, but we have certainly nothing better to put in its place, and for the practical purposes of life monetary calculation as it exists under a sound monetary system always suffices. Were we to dispense with it, any economic system of calculation would become absolutely impossible.

The socialist society would know how to look after itself. It would issue an edict and decide for or against the projected building. Yet this decision would depend at best upon vague estimates; it would never be based upon the foundation of an exact calculation of value.

The static state can dispense with economic calculation. For here the same events in economic life are ever recurring; and if we assume that the first disposition of the static socialist economy follows on the basis of the final state of the competitive economy, we might at all events conceive of a socialist production system which is rationally controlled from an economic point of view. But this is only conceptually possible. For the moment, we leave aside the fact that a static state is impossible in real life, as our economic data are forever changing, so that the static nature of economic activity is only a theoretical assumption corresponding to no real state of affairs, however necessary it may be for our thinking and for the perfection of our knowledge of economics. Even so, we must assume that the transition to socialism must, as a consequence of the levelling out of the differences in income and the resultant readjustments in consumption, and therefore production, change all economic data in such a way that a connecting link with the final state of affairs in the previously existing competitive economy becomes impossible. But then we have the spectacle of a socialist economic order floundering in the ocean of possible and conceivable economic combinations without the compass of economic calculation.

Thus in the socialist commonwealth every economic change becomes an undertaking whose success can be neither appraised in advance nor later retrospectively determined. There is only groping in the dark. Socialism is the abolition of rational economy.

3.
Economic Calculation
in the Socialist Commonwealth

Are we really dealing with the necessary consequences of common ownership of the means of production? Is there no way in which some kind of economic calculation might be tied up with a socialist system?

In every great enterprise, each particular business

or branch of business is to some extent independent in its accounting. It reckons the labor and material against each other, and it is always possible for each individual group to strike a particular balance and to approach the economic results of its activities from an accounting point of view. We can thus ascertain with what success each particular section has labored, and accordingly draw conclusions about the reorganization, curtailment, abandonment, or expansion of existing groups and about the institution of new ones. Admittedly, some mistakes are inevitable in such a calculation. They arise partly from the difficulties consequent upon an allocation of general expenses. Yet other mistakes arise from the necessity of calculating with what are not from many points of view rigorously ascertainable data, e.g. when in the ascertainment of the profitability of a certain method of procedure we compute the amortization of the machines used on the assumption of a given duration for their usefulness. Still, all such mistakes can be confined within certain narrow limits, so that they do not disturb the net result of the calculation. What remains of uncertainty comes into the calculation of the uncertainty of future conditions, which is an inevitable concomitant of the dynamic nature of economic life.

It seems tempting to try to construct by analogy a separate estimation of the particular production groups in the socialist state also. But it is quite impossible. For each separate calculation of the particular branches of one and the same enterprise depends exclusively on the fact that is precisely in market dealings that market prices to be taken as the bases of calculation are formed for all kinds of goods and labor employed. Where there is no free market, there is no pricing mechanism; without a pricing mechanism, there is no economic calculation.

We might conceive of a situation, in which exchange between particular branches of business is permitted, so as to obtain the mechanism of exchange relations (prices) and thus create a basis for economic calculation even in the socialist commonwealth. Within the framework of a uniform economy knowing not private ownership of the means of production, individual labor groups are constituted independent and authoritative disposers, which have indeed to behave in accordance with the directions of the supreme economic council, but which nevertheless assign each other material goods and services only against a payment, which would have to be made in the general medium of exchange. It is roughly in this way that we conceive of the organization of the socialist running of business when we nowadays talk of complete socialization and the like. But we have still not come to the crucial point. Exchange relations between production goods can only be established on the basis of private ownership of the means of production. When the "coal syndicate" provides the "iron syndicate" with coal, no price can be formed, except when both syndicates are the owners of the means of production employed in their business. This would not be socialization but workers' capitalism and syndicalism.

The matter is indeed very simple for those socialist theorists who rely on the labor theory of value.

> As soon as society takes possession of the means of production and applies them to production in their directly socialised form, each individual's labour, however different its specific utility may be, becomes *a priori* and directly social labour. The amount of social labour invested in a product need not then be established indirectly; daily experience immediately tells us how much is necessary on an average. Society can simply calculate how many hours of labour are invested in a steam engine, a quarter of last harvest's wheat, and a 100 yards of linen of given quality ... To be sure, society will also have to know how much labour is needed to produce any consumption-good. It will have to arrange its production plan according to its means of production, to which labour especially belongs. The utility yielded by the various consumption-goods, weighted against each other and against the amount of labour required to produce them, will ultimately determine the plan. People will make everything simple without the mediation of the notorious "value."[9]

Here it is not our task once more to advance critical objections against the labor theory of value. In this connection they can only interest us in so far as they are relevant to an assessment of the applicability of labor in the value computations of a socialist community.

On a first impression calculation in terms of labor also takes into consideration the natural non-human conditions of production. The law of diminishing returns is already allowed for in the concept of socially necessary average labor time to the extent that its operation is due to the variety of the natural conditions of production. If

[9]Friedrich Engels, *Herrn Eugen Dührings Umwälzung des Wissenschaft*, 7th ed., pp. 335 f. [Translated by Emile Burns as *Herr Eugen Dühring's Revolution in Science—Anti-Dühring* (London: Lawrence & Wishart, 1943).]

The Ludwig von Mises Institute • 29

the demand for a commodity increases and worse natural resources must be exploited, then the average socially necessary labor time required for the production of a unit increases too. If more favorable natural resources are discovered, the amount of socially necessary labor diminishes.[10] The consideration of the natural condition of production suffices only in so far as it is reflected in the amount of labor socially necessary. But it is in this respect that valuation in terms of labor fails. It leaves the employment of material factors of production out of account. Let the amount of socially necessary labor time required for the production of each of the commodities P and Q be 10 hours. Further, in addition to labor the production of both P and Q requires the raw material a, a unit of which is produced by an hour's socially necessary labor; 2 units of a and 8 hours' labor are used in the production of P, and one unit of a and 9 hours' labor in the production of Q. In terms of labor P and Q are equivalent, but in value terms P is more valuable than Q. The former is false, and only the latter corresponds to the nature and purpose of calculation. True, this surplus, by which according to value calculation P is more valuable than Q, this material substratum "is given by nature without any addition from man."[11] Still, the fact that it is only present in such quantities that it becomes an object of economizing, must be taken into account in some form or other in value calculation.

[10]Karl Marx, *Capital*, translated by Eden and Cedar Paul (London: Allen & Unwin, 1928), p. 9.

[11]Marx, ibid., p. 12.

The second defect in calculation in terms of labor is the ignoring of the different qualities of labor. To Marx all human labor is economically of the same kind, as it is always "the productive expenditure of human brain, brawn, nerve and hand."[12]

> Skilled labour counts only as intensified, or rather multiplied, simple labour, so that a smaller quantity of skilled labour is equal to a larger quantity of simple labour. Experience shows that skilled labour can always be reduced in this way to the terms of simple labour. No matter that a commodity be the product of the most highly skilled labour, its value can be equated with that of the product of simple labour, so that it represents merely a definite amount of simple labour.

Böhm-Bawerk is not far wrong when he calls this argument "a theoretical juggle of almost stupefying naïveté."[13] To judge Marx's view we need not ask if it is possible to discover a single uniform physiological measure of all human labor, whether it be physical or "mental." For it is certain that there exist among men varying degrees of capacity and dexterity, which cause the products and services of labor to have varying qualities. What must be conclusive in deciding the question whether reckoning in terms of labor is applicable or not, is whether it is or is not possible to bring different kinds

---

[12]Marx, ibid., pp. 13 et seq.

[13]Cf. Eugen von Böhm-Bawerk, *Capital and Interest*, translated by William Smart (London and New York: Macmillan, 1890), p. 384. [See the English translation by George Huncke and Hans F. Sennholz (South Holland, Ill.: Libertarian Press, 1959), p. 299, where the phrase reads "a bit of legerdemain in the theorizing line that is astounding in its naiveté."]

of labor under a common denominator without the mediation of the economic subject's valuation of their products. The proof Marx attempts to give is not successful. Experience indeed shows that goods are consumed under exchange relations without regard of the fact of their being produced by simple or complex labor. But this would only be a proof that given amounts of simple labor are directly made equal to given amounts of complex labor, if it were shown that labor is their source of exchange value. This not only is not demonstrated, but is what Marx is trying to demonstrate by means of these very arguments.

No more is it a proof of this homogeneity that rates of substitution between simple and complex labor are manifested in the wage rate in an exchange economy—a fact to which Marx does not allude in this context. This equalizing process is a result of market transactions and not its antecedent. Calculation in terms of labor would have to set up an arbitrary proportion for the substitution of complex by simple labor, which excludes its employment for purposes of economic administration.

It was long supposed that the labor theory of value was indispensable to socialism, so that the demand for the nationalization of the means of production should have an ethical basis. Today we know this for the error it is. Although the majority of socialist supporters have thus employed this misconception, and although Marx, however much he fundamentally took another point of view, was not altogether free from it, it is clear that the political call for the introduction of socialized production neither requires nor can obtain the support of the labor theory of value on the one hand, and that on the other those people holding different views on the nature and origin of economic value can be socialist according to their sentiments. Yet the labor theory of value is inherently necessary for the supporters of socialist production in a sense other than that usually intended. In the main socialist production might only appear rationally realizable, if it provided an objectively recognizable unit of value, which would permit of economic calculation in an economy where neither money nor exchange were present. And only labor can conceivably be considered as such.

4.

Responsibility and Initiative in Communal Concerns

The problem of responsibility and initiative in socialist enterprises is closely connected with that of economic calculation. It is now universally agreed that the exclusion of free initiative and individual responsibility, on which the successes of private enterprise depend, constitutes the most serious menace to socialist economic organization.[14]

The majority of socialists silently pass this problem

[14]Cf. *Vorläufiger Bericht der Sozialisierungskommission über die Frage der Sozialisierung des Kohlenbergbaues*, concluded 15th February, 1919 (Berlin, 1919), p. 13.

by. Others believe they can answer it with an allusion to the directors of companies; in spite of the fact that they are not the owners of the means of production, enterprises under their control have flourished. If society, instead of company shareholders, becomes the owner of the means of production, nothing will have altered. The directors would not work less satisfactorily for society than for shareholders.

We must distinguish between two groups of joint-stock companies and similar concerns. In the first group, consisting for the large part of smaller companies, a few individuals unite in a common enterprise in the legal form of a company. They are often the heirs of the founders of the company, or often previous competitors who have amalgamated. Here the actual control and management of business is in the hands of the shareholders themselves or at least of some of the shareholders, who do business in their own interest; or in that of closely related shareholders such as wives, minors, etc. The directors in their capacity as members of the board of management or of the board of control, and sometimes also in an attenuated legal capacity, themselves exercise the decisive influence in the conduct of affairs. Nor is this affected by the circumstance that sometimes part of the share-capital is held by a financial consortium or bank. Here in fact the company is only differentiated from the public commercial company by its legal form.

The situation is quite different in the case of large-scale companies, where only a fraction of the shareholders, i.e. the big shareholders, participate in the actual control of the enterprise. And these usually have the same interest in the firm's prosperity as any property holder. Still, it may well be that they have interests other than those of the vast majority of small shareholders, who are excluded from the management even if they own the larger part of the share-capital. Severe collisions may occur, when the firm's business is so handled on behalf of the directors that the shareholders are injured. But be that as it may, it is clear that the real holders of power in companies run the business in their own interest, whether it coincides with that of the shareholders or not. In the long run it will generally be to the advantage of the solid company administrator, who is not merely bent on making a transient profit, to represent the shareholders' interests only in every case and to avoid manipulations which might damage them. This holds good in the first instance for banks and financial groups, which should not trifle at the public's expense with the credit they enjoy. Thus it is not merely on the prescriptiveness of ethical motives that the success of companies depends.

The situation is completely transformed when an undertaking is nationalized. The motive force disappears with the exclusion of the material interests of private individuals, and if State and municipal enterprises thrive at all, they owe it to the taking over of "management" from private enterprise, or to the fact that they are ever driven to reforms and innovations by the business men from whom they purchase their instruments of production and raw material.

Since we are in a position to survey decades of State and socialist endeavor, it is now generally recognized that there is no internal pressure to reform and improvement of production in socialist undertakings, that they cannot be adjusted to the changing conditions of demand, and that in a word they are a dead limb in the economic organism. All attempts to breathe life into them have so far been in vain. It was supposed that a reform in the system of remuneration might achieve the desired end. If the managers of these enterprises were interested in the yield, it was thought they would be in a position comparable to that of the manager of large-scale companies. This is a fatal error. The managers of large-scale companies are bound up with the interests of the businesses they administer in an entirely different way from what could be the case in public concerns. They are either already owners of a not inconsiderable fraction of the share capital, or hope to become so in due course. Further, they are in a position to obtain profits by stock exchange speculation in the company's shares. They have the prospect of bequeathing their positions to, or at least securing part of their influence for, their heirs. The type to which the success of joint-stock companies is to be attributed, is not that of a complacently prosperous managing director resembling the civil servant in his outlook and experience; rather it is precisely the manager, promoter, and man of affairs, who is himself interested as a shareholder, whom it is the aim of all nationalization and municipalization to exclude.

It is not generally legitimate to appeal in a socialist context to such arguments in order to ensure the success of an economic order built on socialist foundations. All socialist systems, including that of Karl Marx, and his orthodox supporters, proceed from the assumption that in a socialist society a conflict between the interests of the particular and general could not possibly arise. Everybody will act in his own interest in giving of his best because he participates in the product of all economic activity. The obvious objection that the individual is very little concerned whether he himself is diligent and enthusiastic, and that it is of greater moment to him that everybody else should be, is either completely ignored or is insufficiently dealt with by them. They believe they can construct a socialist commonwealth on the basis of the Categorical Imperative alone. How lightly it is their wont to proceed in this way is best shown by Kautsky when he says, "If socialism is a social necessity, then it would be human nature and not socialism which would have to readjust itself, if ever the two clashed."[15] This is nothing but sheer Utopianism.

But even if we for the moment grant that these Utopian expectations can actually be realized, that each individual in a socialist society will exert himself with the same zeal as he does today in a society where he is subjected to the pressure of free competition, there still remains the problem of measuring the result of economic activity in a socialist commonwealth which does not permit of any economic calculation. We cannot act economically if we are not in a position to understand economizing.

[15]Cf. Karl Kautsky, Preface to "Atlanticus" [Gustav Jaeckh], *Produktion und Konsum im Sozialstaat* (Stuttgart: J. H. W. Dietz, 1898), p. 14.

A popular slogan affirms that if we think less bureaucratically and more commercially in communal enterprises, they will work just as well as private enterprises. The leading positions must be occupied by merchants, and then income will grow apace. Unfortunately "commercial-mindedness" is not something external, which can be arbitrarily transferred. A merchant's qualities are not the property of a person depending on inborn aptitude, nor are they acquired by studies in a commercial school or by working in a commercial house, or even by having been a business man oneself for some period of time. The entrepreneur's commercial attitude and activity arises from his position in the economic process and is lost with its disappearance. When a successful business man is appointed the manager of a public enterprise, he may still bring with him certain experiences from his previous occupation, and be able to turn them to good account in a routine fashion for some time. Still, with his entry into communal activity he ceases to be a merchant and becomes as much a bureaucrat as any other placeman in the public employ. It is not a knowledge of bookkeeping, of business organization, or of the style of commercial correspondence, or even a dispensation from a commercial high school, which makes the merchant, but his characteristic position in the production process, which allows of the identification of the firm's and his own interests. It is no solution of the problem when Otto Bauer in his most recently published work proposes that the directors of the National Central Bank, on whom leadership in the economic process will be conferred, should be nominated by a Collegium, to which representatives of the teaching staff of the commercial high schools would also belong.[16] Like Plato's philosophers, the directors so appointed may well be the wisest and best of their kind, but they cannot be merchants in their posts as leaders of a socialist society, even if they should have been previously.

It is a general complaint that the administration of public undertakings lacks initiative. It is believed that this might be remedied by changes in organization. This also is a grievous mistake. The management of a socialist concern cannot entirely be placed in the hands of a single individual, because there must always be the suspicion that he will permit errors inflicting heavy damages on the community. But if the important conclusions are made dependent on the votes of committees, or on the consent of the relevant government offices, then limitations are imposed on the individual's initiative. Committees are rarely inclined to introduce bold innovations. The lack of free initiative in public business rests not on an absence of organization, it is inherent in the nature of the business itself. One cannot transfer free disposal of the factors of production to an employee, however high his rank, and this becomes even less possible, the more strongly he is materially interested in the successful performance of his duties; for in practice the propertyless manager can only be held morally responsible for

---

[16]Cf. Otto Bauer, *Der Weg zum Sozialismus* (Vienna: Ignaz Brand, 1919), p. 25.

losses incurred. And so ethical losses are juxtaposed with opportunities for material gain. The property owner on the other hand himself bears responsibility, as he himself must primarily feel the loss arising from unwisely conducted business. It is precisely in this that there is a characteristic difference between liberal and socialist production.

5.
The Most Recent Socialist Doctrines and the Problem of Economic Calculation

Since recent events helped socialist parties to obtain power in Russia, Hungary, Germany and Austria, and have thus made the execution of a socialist nationalization program a topical issue,[17] Marxist writers have themselves begun to deal more closely with the problems of the regulation of the socialist commonwealth. But even now they still cautiously avoid the crucial question, leaving it to be tackled by the despised "Utopians." They themselves prefer to confine their attention to what is to be done in the immediate future; they are forever drawing up programs of the path to Socialism and not of Socialism itself. The only possible conclusion from all these writings is that they are not even conscious of the larger problem of economic calculation in a socialist society.

[17][The reader will remember that Mises is writing in 1920.]

To Otto Bauer the nationalization of the banks appears the final and decisive step in the carrying through of the socialist nationalization program. If all banks are nationalized and amalgamated into a single central bank, then its administrative board becomes "the supreme economic authority, the chief administrative organ of the whole economy. Only by nationalization of the banks does society obtain the power to regulate its labor according to a plan, and to distribute its resources rationally among the various branches of production, so as to adapt them to the nation's needs."[18] Bauer is not discussing the monetary arrangements which will prevail in the socialist commonwealth after the completion of the nationalization of the banks. Like other Marxists he is trying to show how simply and obviously the future socialist order of society will evolve from the conditions prevailing in a developed capitalist economy. "It suffices to transfer to the nation's representatives the power now exercised by bank shareholders through the Administrative Boards they elect,"[19] in order to socialize the banks and thus to lay the last brick on the edifice of socialism. Bauer leaves his readers completely ignorant of the fact that the nature of the banks is entirely changed in the process of nationalization and amalgamation into one central bank. Once the banks merge into a single bank, their essence is wholly transformed; they are then in a position to issue credit without any limitation.[20] In this

[18]Bauer, op cit., pp. 26 f.

[19]Ibid., p. 25.

[20]Mises, op. cit., pp. 474 ff. [Compare p. 411 of the 1980 English edition, op. cit.]

fashion the monetary system as we know it today disappears of itself. When in addition the single central bank is nationalized in a society, which is otherwise already completely socialized, market dealings disappear and all exchange transactions are abolished. At the same time the Bank ceases to be a bank, its specific functions are extinguished, for there is no longer any place for it in such a society. It may be that the name "Bank" is retained, that the Supreme Economic Council of the socialist community is called the Board of Directors of the Bank, and that they hold their meetings in a building formerly occupied by a bank. But it is no longer a bank, it fulfils none of those functions which a bank fulfils in an economic system resting on the private ownership of the means of production and the use of a general medium of exchange—money. It no longer distributes any credit, for a socialist society makes credit of necessity impossible. Bauer himself does not tell us what a bank is, but he begins his chapter on the nationalization of the banks with the sentence: "All disposable capital flows into a common pool in the banks."[21] As a Marxist must he not raise the question of what the banks' activities will be after the abolition of capitalism?

All other writers who have grappled with the problems of the organization of the socialist commonwealth are guilty of similar confusions. They do not realize that the bases of economic calculation are removed by the exclusion of exchange and the pricing mechanism, and that

[21]Bauer, op. cit., p. 24.

something must be substituted in its place, if all economy is not to be abolished and a hopeless chaos is not to result. People believe that socialist institutions might evolve without further ado from those of a capitalist economy. This is not at all the case. And it becomes all the more grotesque when we talk of banks, banks management, etc. in a socialist commonwealth.

Reference to the conditions that have developed in Russia and Hungary under Soviet rule proves nothing. What we have there is nothing but a picture of the destruction of an existing order of social production, for which a closed peasant household economy has been substituted. All branches of production depending on social division of labor are in a state of entire dissolution. What is happening under the rule of Lenin and Trotsky is merely destruction and annihilation. Whether, as the liberals[22] hold, socialism must inevitably draw these consequences in its train, or whether, as the socialists retort, this is only a result of the fact that the Soviet Republic is attacked from without, is a question of no interest to us in this context. All that has to be established is the fact that the Soviet socialist commonwealth has not even begun to discuss the problem of economic calculation, nor has it any cause to do so. For where things are still produced for the market in Soviet Russia in spite of governmental prohibitions, they

---

[22][Mises is using the term "liberal" here in its nineteenth-century European sense, meaning "classical liberal" or libertarian. On liberalism see Mises's *Liberalism: In the Classical Tradition*, translated by Ralph Raico (Irvington-on-Hudson, N.Y.: Foundation for Economic Education, 1985).]

are valued in terms of money, for there exists to that extent private ownership of the means of production, and goods are sold against money. Even the Government cannot deny the necessity, which it confirms by increasing the amount of money in circulation, of retaining a monetary system for at least the transition period.

That the essence of the problem to be faced has not yet come to light in Soviet Russia, Lenin's statements in his essay on *Die nächsten Aufgaben der Sowjetmacht* best show. In the dictator's deliberations there ever recurs the thought that the immediate and most pressing task of Russian communism is "the organization of bookkeeping and control of those concerns, in which the capitalists have already been expropriated, and of all other economic concerns."[23] Even so Lenin is far from realizing that an entirely new problem is here involved which it is impossible to solve with the conceptual instruments of "bourgeois" culture. Like a real politician, he does not bother with issues beyond his nose. He still finds himself surrounded by monetary transactions, and does not notice that with progressive socialization money also necessarily loses its function as the medium of exchange in general use, to the extent that private property and with it exchange disappear. The implication of Lenin's reflections is that he would like to re-introduce into Soviet

---

[23]Cf. V. I. Lenin, *Die nächsten Aufgaben der Sowjetmacht* (Berlin: Wilmersdorf, 1919), pp. 12 f., 22 ff. [English translation, *The Soviets at Work.*—This edition.]

business "bourgeois" bookkeeping carried on on a monetary basis. Therefore he also desires to restore "bourgeois experts" to a state of grace.[24] For the rest Lenin is as little aware as Bauer of the fact that in a socialist commonwealth the functions of the bank are unthinkable in their existing sense. He wishes to go farther with the "nationalization of the banks" and to proceed "to a transformation of the banks into the nodal point of social bookkeeping under socialism."[25]

Lenin's ideas on the socialist economic system, to which he is striving to lead his people, are generally obscure.

> "The socialist state," he says "can only arise as a net of producing and consuming communes, which conscientiously record their production and consumption, go about their labour economically, uninterruptedly raise their labour productivity and thus attain the possibility of lowering the working day to seven or six hours or even lower."[26] "Every factor, every village appears as a production and consumption commune having the right and obligation to apply the general Soviet legislation in its own way ('in its own way' not in the sense of its violation but in the sense of the variety of its forms of realisation), and to solve in its own way the problems of calculating the production and distribution of products."[27]

"The chief communes must and will serve the most

[24]Op. cit., p. 15.

[25]Ibid., pp. 21 and 26. Compare also Bukharin, *Das Programm der Kommunisten* (Zürich: no pub., 1918), pp. 27 ff.

[26]Cf. Lenin, op. cit., pp. 24 f.

[27]Ibid., p. 32.

backward ones as educators, teachers, and stimulating leaders." The successes of the chief communes must be broadcast in all their details in order to provide a good example. The communes "showing good business results" should be immediately rewarded "by a curtailment of the working day and with an increase in wages, and by allowing more attention to be paid to cultural and aesthetic goods and values."[28]

We can infer that Lenin's ideal is a state of society in which the means of production are not the property of a few districts, municipalities, or even of the workers in the concern, but of the whole community. His ideal is socialist and not syndicalist. This need not be specially stressed for a Marxist such as Lenin. It is not extraordinary of Lenin the theorist, but of Lenin the statesman, who is the leader of the syndicalist and small-holding peasant Russian revolution. However, at the moment we are engaged with the writer Lenin and may consider his ideals separately, without letting ourselves be disturbed by the picture of sober reality. According to Lenin the theorist, every large agricultural and industrial concern is a member of the great commonwealth of labor. Those who are active in this commonwealth have the right of self-government; they exercise a profound influence on the direction of production and again on the distribution of the goods they are assigned for consumption. Still labor is the property of the whole society, and as its product belongs to society also, it therefore disposes of its distribution. How, we

[28]Ibid., p. 33.

must now ask, is calculation in the economy carried on in a socialist commonwealth which is so organized? Lenin gives us a most inadequate answer by referring us back to statistics. We must

> bring statistics to the masses, make it popular, so that the active population will gradually learn by themselves to understand and realize how much and what kind of work must be done, how much and what kind of recreation should be taken, so that the comparison of the economy's industrial results in the case of individual communes becomes the object of general interest and education.[29]

From these scanty allusions it is impossible to infer what Lenin understands by statistics and whether he is thinking of monetary or *in natura* computation. In any case, we must refer back to what we have said about the impossibility of learning the money prices of production-goods in a socialist commonwealth and about the difficulties standing in the way of *in natura* valuation.[30] Statistics would only be applicable to economic calculation if it could go beyond the *in natura* calculation, whose ill-suitedness for this purpose we have demonstrated. It is naturally impossible where no exchange relations are formed between goods in the process of trade.

---

[29]Op. cit., p. 33.

[30]Neurath, too (cf. op. cit., pp. 212 et seq.), imputes great importance to statistics for the setting up of the socialist economic plan.

Conclusion

It must follow from what we have been able to establish in our previous arguments that the protagonists of a socialist system of production claim preference for it on the ground of greater rationality as against an economy so constituted as to depend on private ownership of the means of production. We have no need to consider this opinion within the framework of the present essay, in so far as it falls back on the assertion that rational economic activity necessarily cannot be perfect, because certain forces are operative which hinder its pursuance. In this connection we may only pay attention to the economic and technical reason for this opinion. There hovers before the holders of this tenet a muddled conception of technical rationality, which stands in antithesis to economic rationality, on which also they are not very clear. They are wont to overlook the fact that "all technical rationality of production is identical with a low level of specific expenditure in the processes of production."[31] They overlook the fact that technical calculation is not enough to realize the "degree of general and teleological expediency"[32] of an event; that it can only grade individual events according to their significance; but that it can never guide us in those judgments which are demanded by the economic complex as a whole. Only because of the fact that technical considerations can be based on profitability can we

[31]Cf. Gottl, op. cit., p. 220.

[32]Ibid., p. 219.

overcome the difficulty arising from the complexity of the relations between the mighty system of present-day production on the one hand and demand and the efficiency of enterprises and economic units on the other; and can we gain the complete picture of the situation in its totality, which rational economic activity requires.[33]

These theories are dominated by a confused conception of the primacy of objective use value. In fact, so far as economic administration is concerned, objective use value can only acquire significance for the economy through the influence it derives from subjective use value on the formation of the exchange relations of economic goods. A second confused idea is inexplicably involved—the observer's personal judgment of the utility of goods as opposed to the judgments of the people participating in economic transactions. If anyone finds it "irrational" to spend as much as is expended in society on smoking, drinking, and similar enjoyments, then doubtless he is right from the point of view of his own personal scale of values. But in so judging, he is ignoring the fact that economy is a means, and that, without prejudice to the rational considerations influencing its pattern, the scale of ultimate ends is a matter for conation and not for cognition.

The knowledge of the fact that rational economic activity is impossible in a socialist commonwealth cannot, of course, be used as an argument either for or against

---

[33]Ibid., p. 225.

socialism. Whoever is prepared himself to enter upon socialism on ethical grounds on the supposition that the provision of goods of a lower order for human beings under a system of common ownership of the means of production is diminished, or whoever is guided by ascetic ideals in his desire for socialism, will not allow himself to be influenced in his endeavors by what we have said. Still less will those "culture" socialists be deterred who, like Muckle, expect from socialism primarily "the dissolution of the most frightful of all barbarisms—capitalist rationality."[34] But he who expects a rational economic system from socialism will be forced to re-examine his views.

---

[34]Cf. Friedrich Muckle, *Das Kulturideal des Sozialismus* (Munich and Leipzig: Duncker & Humblot, 1919), p. 213. On the other hand, Muckle demands the "highest degree of rationalisation of economic life in order to curtail hours of labour, and to permit man to withdraw to an island where he can listen to the melody of his being."

Postscript:

Why a Socialist Economy is "Impossible"

Mises's Thesis

In "Economic Calculation in the Socialist Common-wealth," Ludwig von Mises demonstrates, once and forever, that, under socialist central planning, there are no means of economic calculation and that, therefore, socialist economy itself is "impossible" ("unmöglich")— not just inefficient or less innovative or conducted without benefit of decentralized knowledge, but really and truly and literally *impossible.*

At the same time, he establishes that the necessary and sufficient conditions of the existence and evolution of human society are liberty, property, and sound money: the liberty of each individual to produce and exchange according to independently formed value judgments and price appraisements; unrestricted private ownership of all types and orders of producer goods as well as of consumer goods; and the existence of a universal medium of exchange whose value is not subject to large or unforeseeable variations.

Abolish all or even one of these institutions and human society disintegrates amid a congeries of isolated household economies and predatory tribes. But not only does abolition of private ownership of the means of production by a world-embracing socialist state render human social existence impossible: Mises's analysis also implies that socialism destroys the praxeological significance of time and nullifies humanity's uniquely teleological contribution to the universe.

Because Mises's critique of socialism has been the subject of significant misinterpretation by his followers as well as his opponents, his argument, as it is presented in this article, should be restated.

The Calculation Argument

(1) Mises's pathbreaking and central insight is that monetary calculation is the indispensable mental tool for choosing the optimum among the vast array of intricately-related production plans that are available for employing the factors of production within the framework of the social division of labor. Without recourse to calculating and comparing the benefits and costs of production using the structure of monetary prices determined at each moment on the market, the human mind is only capable of surveying, evaluating, and directing production processes whose scope is drastically restricted to the compass of the primitive household economy.

The practically unlimited number of alternative plans for allocating the factors of production and the overwhelming complexities of their interrelationships stem from two related facts about our world. First, our world is endowed with a wide variety of relatively "nonspecific" resources, which to a greater or lesser degree are substitutable for one another over a broad range of production processes. Second, since human action itself implies the ineradicable scarcity of time as well as of resources, there always exists an almost inexhaustible opportunity to accumulate capital and lengthen the economy's structure of production, thus multiplying beyond number the technical possibilities for combining the factors of production.

Given, therefore, the infinitude of the relationships of complementarity and substitutability simultaneously subsisting among the various types of productive resources, a single human mind—even if it were miraculously endowed with complete and accurate knowledge of the quantities and qualities of the available factors of production, of the latest techniques for combining and transforming these factors into consumer goods, and of the set of all individuals' value rankings of consumer goods—would be utterly incapable of determining the optimal pattern of resource allocation or even if a particular plan were ludicrously and destructively uneconomic. Not only would this perfectly knowledgeable person be unable to devise a rational solution of the problem, he or she would be unable to even achieve a full intellectual "survey" of the problem in all its complexity.

Thus, as Mises (p. 17) says, "...the mind of one man alone—be it never so cunning, is too weak to grasp the importance of any single one among the countlessly many goods of a higher order. No single man can ever master all the possibilities of production, innumerable as they are, as to be in a position to make straightway evident judgments of value without the aid of some system of computation."

(2) What is needed, then, to produce the cardinal numbers necessary for computing the costs and benefits of production processes is what Mises (p. 19) calls the "intellectual division of labor" which emerges when private property owners are at liberty to exchange goods and services against money according to their individual value judgments and price appraisements. Thus in a market society every individual mind is accorded a dual role in determining the quantities of monetary calculation. In their consumer roles, all people make monetary bids for the existing stocks of final goods according to their subjective valuations, leading to the emergence of objective monetary exchange ratios which relate the values of all consumer goods to one another.

In light of the system of consumer goods' prices thus determined, and of the existing knowledge of the technical conditions of production, entrepreneurs seeking to maximize monetary profit bid against one another to acquire the services of the productive factors currently available and owned by these same consumers (including those in entrepreneurial roles). In this competitive process, each and every type of productive service is objectively appraised in monetary terms according to its ultimate contribution to the production of consumer goods. There thus comes into being the market's monetary price structure, a genuinely "social" phenomenon in which every unit of exchangeable goods and services is assigned a socially significant cardinal number and which has its roots in the minds of every single member of society yet must forever transcend the contribution of the individual human mind.

(3) Since the social price structure is continually being destroyed and recreated at every moment of time by the competitive appraisement process operating in the face of ceaseless change of the economic data, there is always available to entrepreneurs the means of estimating the costs and revenues and calculating the profitability of any thinkable process of production.

Once private property in the nonhuman means of production is abolished, however, as it is under socialism, the appraisement process must grind to a halt, leaving only the increasingly irrelevant memory of the market's final price structure. In the absence of competitive bidding for productive resources by entrepreneurs, there is no possibility of assigning economic meaning to the amalgam of potential physical productivities embodied in each of the myriad of natural resources and capital goods now in the hands of the socialist central planners.

Even if planners observed the money prices which continued to be generated on an unhampered market for consumer goods, or substituted their own unitary scale of values for those of their subject consumers, there would still be no possibility for the central planners to ever know or guess the "opportunity cost" of any social production process. Where actors, in principle, are not in a position to compare the estimated costs and benefits of their decisions, economizing activities, by definition, are ruled out.

A society without monetary calculation, that is, a

socialist society, is therefore quite literally a society without an economy. Thus, contrary to what has become the conventional interpretation by friend and foe alike, Mises (pp. 21 and 26) was not indulging in rhetorical hyperbole but drily stating a demonstrable conclusion of economic science when he declared in this article: "Without economic calculation there can be no economy. Hence in a socialist state wherein the pursuit of economic calculation is impossible, there can be—in our sense of the term—no economy whatsoever ... Socialism is the abolition of rational economy."

(4) Socialism will have particularly devastating effects on the economy's capital structure. Without a unitary expression for time preferences in monetary terms, central planners will never know whether the investment of current resources in the higher stages of production, which yield physically heterogeneous and noncommensurable outputs, will generate an overall production structure whose parts fit together or whose intended length is adjusted to the amount of capital available. Thus higher-order technical processes will be undertaken whose outputs cannot be used in further production processes because the needed complementary producer goods are not available.

In the Soviet Union, for example, in the midst of a dire undersupply of food products, new and unused tractors stand rusting in fields of unharvested grain, because there does not exist sufficient fuel to power them, labor to operate them, or structures to house them. One of the most important consequences of the fact that centrally planned economies exist within a world market economy is that the planners can observe and crudely copy capitalist economies in deciding which technical processes can coexist in a reasonably coherent capital structure. Had the entire world, rather than isolated nations, existed under central planning for the last half century, the global capital structure would long since have crumbled irretrievably to dust and humanity been catapulted back to autarkic primitivism.

(5) Thus, from the first, Mises emphasized the point, which was conveniently ignored by hostile and disingenuous critics, that the existence of the Soviet Union and other centrally-controlled economies is no refutation of his thesis regarding the impossibility of socialist economy. Their gross inefficiency notwithstanding, these economies in fact do eke out a precarious existence as parasites on the social appraisement process and integrated capital structure produced by the surrounding world market. As Mises (p. 20) points out, neither these economies nor nationalized enterprises within capitalist economies are genuinely socialistic, because both entities

> are so much dependent upon the environing economic system with its free commerce that they cannot be said to partake ... of the really essential nature of a socialist economy.... In state and municipal undertakings technical improvements are introduced because their effect in similar private enterprises, domestic and foreign, can be noticed, and because those private industries which produce the materials for these improvements give the impulse for their introduction. In these concerns the advantages of reorganization can be established, because they operate within the sphere of a

society based upon the private ownership of the means of production and upon the system of monetary exchange, being thus capable of computation and account.

(6) But Mises does not stop with the demonstration that socialism must eradicate economizing activity within the social nexus; he also traces out its implications for the development of the human mind. With the dissolution of social production that inevitably ensues upon the imposition of a world-embracing socialist state, humanity is reduced in short order to dependence upon economic activities carried on in relative isolation. The primitive production processes suitable to autarkic economies do not require economic calculation using cardinal numbers nor do such simple processes offer much scope for purely technical calculation. No longer dependent upon arithmetic operations to sustain itself, the human mind begins to lose its characteristic ability to calculate.

Mises's analysis of the effects of socialism also has another momentous implication. With the impossibility of building up and maintaining a capital structure in the absence of monetary calculation, human economy under socialism comes to consist of super-short and repetitive household processes utilizing minimal capital and with little scope for adjustment to new wants. The result is that time itself—in the praxeological sense of a distinction between present and future—ceases to play a role in human affairs. Men and women, in their capitalless, hand-to-mouth existence, begin to passively experience time as the brute beasts do—not actively as a tool of planning and action but passively as mere duration. Humanity as a teleological force in the universe is therefore necessarily a creation of the inextricably related phenomena of calculation and capital. In a meaningful sense, then, socialism not only exterminates economy and society but the human intellect and spirit as well.

Mises vs. the Hayekians

(1) It is of utmost importance to recognize that, in his original article as well as all later writings on the subject, Mises unswervingly identified the unique and insoluble problem of socialism as the impossibility of calculation—not, as in the case of F. A. Hayek, as an absence of an efficient mechanism for conveying knowledge to the planners. This difference between Mises and Hayek is reflected in their respective conceptions of the social function of competition as well as in their responses to the claims of the later market and mathematical socialists. Actually, Mises anticipated and refuted both groups in his original article. Nonetheless, Mises's position on these issues is today generally ignored or conflated with Hayek's.

(2) For Mises, the starting point for entrepreneurial planning of production in a market economy is the experience of the present (actually immediately past) price structure of the market as well as of the underlying economic data. Knowledge of past market prices by the entrepreneur does not substitute for qualitative information about the economy, as Hayek seems to argue, but is necessarily complementary to it. The reason, for Mises, is that it is

price structures as they emerge at future moments of time that are relevant to unavoidably time-consuming and therefore future-oriented production plans. But entrepreneurs can never know future prices directly; they are only able to *appraise* them in light of their "experience" of past prices and of their "understanding" of what transformations will take place in the present configuration of the qualitative economic data. Whether or not one prefers to characterize entrepreneurial forecasting and appraisement as a procedure for "discovery" of knowledge, as Hayek does, what is important is that for Mises it is the indispensable starting point of the competitive process and not its social culminant.

In other words, the forecasting and appraisement of future price structures in which discovery of new knowledge may be said to play a role is a *precompetitive* and *nonsocial* operation, that is, it precedes and conditions competitive entrepreneurial bidding for existing factors of production and is carried on wholly within the compass of individual minds. The *social* function of competition, on the other hand, is the objective price appraisement of the higher-order goods, the *sine qua non* of entrepreneurial calculation of the profitability of alternative production plans. Competition therefore acquires the characteristic of a quintessentially social process, not because its operation presupposes knowledge discovery, which is inescapably an individual function, but because, in the absence of competitively determined money prices for the factors of production, possession of literally all the knowledge in the world would not enable an individual to allocate productive resources economically within the social division of labor.

(3) Mises thus assumes in all his writings on the subject that the planners have full knowledge of consumer valuations of final goods as well as of the various means available for producing these goods under known technological conditions. For example, Mises (p. 23) writes, "The administration may know exactly what goods are most urgently needed.... It may also be able to calculate the value of any means of production by calculating the consequence of its withdrawal in relation to the satisfaction of needs." Despite this knowledge, the socialist administrators would be unable to arrive at a useful social appraisement of the means of production in cardinal terms. This can only occur where there exists private ownership and exchange of productive resources, which generates catallactic competition among independent producers resulting in the imputation of meaningful money prices to the resources.

(4) Anticipating the future arguments of market socialists, Mises reasons that any attempt to implement monetary calculation by forcing or inducing managers of socialist enterprises to act as profit-maximizing (or even more absurdly, price-and-marginal-cost-equalizing) entrepreneurs founders on the fact that these managers do not have an ownership interest in the capital and output of their enterprises. Consequently, the bids they make against one another in seeking to acquire investment funds and purchase productive resources must result in interest rates and prices that are wholly and inescapably arbitrary and useless as tools of economic calculation.

The meaninglessness of these so-called "parametric prices" of market socialism, and their failure to replicate the price structure of the market, derive from the circumstance that they are wholly conditioned by the system of rewards and penalties and other arrangements instituted by the monopoly owners of the factors of production (the planners) to guide the behavior of their managers. But this system of managerial incentives is itself a construct of the individual human mind, which would first have to solve for itself the problem of valuing the factors of production before it could even hope to devise the proper (but now superfluous) incentive structure.

(5) Hayek and his followers are skeptical regarding how quickly and effectively dispersed knowledge of the changing economic circumstances can be incorporated into the socialist price system. But for Mises's analysis, this is quite beside the point. Regardless of how well-informed the socialist managers are, their bids in the "market" for factors of production, to which the central planners are supposed to adjust the price parameters of the system, emerge from an arbitrary set of directives from the planners themselves and not from competition among private property owners. The prices could be no more useless for the task of economic calculation, if the planners eschewed the elaborate and wasteful charade of orchestrating a pseudo-market and simply picked them out of a hat.

(6) From the Misesian point of view, moreover, the shortcomings of the prices of market socialism do not stem from the fact that such prices are supposed to be treated

as "parametric" by the managers, as has been curiously argued recently by some of Mises's followers. The problem is precisely that such prices are *not* genuinely parametric from the point of view of all members of the social body. The prices which emerge on the free market are meaningful for economic calculation because and to the extent that they are determined by a social appraisement process, which, though it is the inevitable outcome of the mental operations of all consumers and producers, yet enters as an unalterable external factor in the buying and selling plans of every individual actor.

(7) In the 1930s, Hayek and the British Misesian Lionel (later Lord) Robbins made a fateful and wholly unwarranted concession to those who contended that the methods of mathematical economics could be successfully bent to yield a solution for the socialist calculation problem. In response to the argument that prices of the factors of production would emerge from the solution of a set of simultaneous equations which incorporated the given data of the economic system, Hayek and Robbins argued that in "theory" this was true but in "practice," highly problematic.

The reason for its impracticality, according to Hayek and Robbins, is that, in the real-world economy, consumer wants, available resources, and technology are subject to continual and unforeseeable change. Therefore, by the time the planners had assembled the vast amount of information needed to formulate the massive equation system and succeeded in solving it (manually or mechanically, since there were no high-speed computers in the 1930s), the system of prices which emerged would be completely inapplicable to the current economy, whose underlying data had changed rapidly and unpredictably in the meantime.

Unfortunately, the Hayek-Robbins response was construed by most economists to mean that the theoretical debate over socialist calculation had come to an end with the concession from the Misesian side that socialism could calculate after all, though perhaps a day late in practice. Moreover, some contemporary Austrian writers, in a belated effort to reclaim the theoretical high ground, have reconstructed the case against socialism along lines suggested by Hayek's later articles on knowledge and competition, which, for all their subtle and compelling argumentation, are disturbingly quasi-Walrasian, seemingly disregarding the lapse of time between present and future prices. The result has been an unacknowledged but momentous retreat from the original and unrefuted Misesian critique emphasizing the absolute impossibility of economic calculation without market prices to a categorically different Hayekian position criticizing the relative inefficiency of non-market mechanisms for discovery, communication, and use of knowledge in the allocation of productive resources.

(8) In sharp contrast to the Hayek-Robbins rejoinder and the reconstructed Austrian critique, Mises's neglected refutation of the mathematical socialists, which is outlined in his original article (pp. 25-26) and elaborated upon in *Human Action*, does not deviate in the slightest from the fundamental and crucial calculation perspective. Thus Mises assumes that the economic data underlying an

existing market economy are suddenly and forever frozen and revealed to newly appointed central planners.

With brilliant insight, Mises demonstrates that, even with Hayekian knowledge problems thus banished from consideration, the planners would still be unable to calculate the optimal or any pattern of deployment for the factors of production. The reason is that the existing capital structure and acquired skills and locations of the labor force are initially maladjusted to the newly prevailing equilibrium configuration of the data. The planners therefore would be forced to decide how to allocate the flow of productive services among the myriads of potential technical production processes and labor retraining and relocation projects so as to secure the optimal path of adjustment to equilibrium for the existing stocks of capital goods, labor skills, and housing. The bewildering complexity of this allocation decision rests on the fact that the planners will be confronted with altered conditions *at every moment of time* during this disequilibrium transition process, since the quantities and qualities of the available productive services themselves are in constant flux due to the circumstance that they originate in the very stocks of physical assets and labor skills that are being progressively transformed.

(9) Complicating this problem beyond conception is the added fact that the leveling of incomes under the new socialist regime and the inevitable fluctuation of current incomes attending the transformation of the production structure would effect a continual revolution in the structure of consumer demands during the transition period.

Mises (p. 26) is surely not overstating his case when he concludes that "... the transition to socialism must ... change all economic data in such a way that a connecting link with the final state of affairs in the previously existent competitive economy becomes impossible. But then we have the spectacle of a socialist economic order floundering in the ocean of possible and conceivable economic combinations without the compass of economic calculation."

Even if mathematics, therefore, yields a consistent set of prices for the given data of equilibrium, this solution is inapplicable to the calculation problems of the dynamic approach to equilibrium. In this situation, use of such prices to allocate resources does not allow the economy to achieve equilibrium, at any rate, before the capital structure and the entire system of social production is demolished.

Thus Mises's original thesis stands on its own against all counterarguments and without any need for qualification or emendation: without private ownership of the means of production, and catallactic competition for them, there cannot exist economic calculation and rational allocation of resources under conditions of the social division of labor. In short, socialist economy and society are impossible.

Beyond Socialism

(1) But though Mises's thesis may remain valid, is it still relevant in a world in which socialist planned economies have collapsed like a house of cards? The answer is a

resounding "yes," for Mises's argument (p. 20) implies that "Every step that takes us away from private ownership of the means of production and from the use of money also takes us away from rational economics."

The never-ending growth of the bloated, rapacious, unjust, and unlovely American and other Western-style welfare states involves an ongoing series of such steps. Looking at it from another angle, the blessedly defunct planned economies of Eastern Europe, as noted above, were far from being genuinely socialist economies in the Misesian sense, because of their ability to trade in and observe the capital complementarities and prices of the world market. They were, and the Soviet Union, China, and others still are, gigantic monopoloid entities that suppress internal markets for capital goods yet maintain subjective and objective relationships with the world market order which enables them to crudely calculate their actions.

As the parasitic welfare state expands its power of monetary inflation and of regulating and intervening into its host "mixed" economy, we can expect productive activities to become more chaotic and guided less and less by socially-determined market prices. In fact, long before a state of complete socialization is achieved, economy and society will begin to disintegrate amid failure of markets to clear, increasing barter, less efficient sizes and forms of business organizations, misallocation and technical inefficiency of productive resources, and disastrous declines of gross capital investment, labor productivity, and living standards. The dangers currently threatening to plunge sectors of the U. S. economy into calculational chaos can be illustrated with a few examples.

(2) Let us consider inflation. One of the most important factors operating to restrain governments of the United States and other mixed economies from reinstituting the inflationary monetary policies which brought us the double-digit rates of price increase of the 1970s is the coexistence of closely integrated global capital markets and independent national fiat currencies issued by central banks jealous of their prerogatives. Any nation that attempts a highly inflationary monetary policy courts the prospect of a rapidly depreciating exchange rate for its currency, a "flight" of investors from its domestic capital market, and a stratospheric climb in interest rates. In the current jargon, monetary authorities, even of large nations such as the United States, have "lost control of domestic interest rates."

Now, there is a much ballyhooed movement afoot to effect greater international "coordination" of monetary and fiscal policies or even to introduce a supranational central bank empowered to issue its own fiat currency. At bottom, such proposals seek to loosen the restraints on monetary inflation at the domestic level and allow politicians and bureaucrats and their allied special interests to surreptitiously extract an expanding flow of lucre or "welfare" from the productive sectors of their economies.

More importantly from our point of view, these international monetary arrangements greatly increase the threat of hyperinflation and the consequent disintegration of the world market economy. Moreover, even if it were reined in before hiving off into hyper-inflationary currency collapse, a bout of galloping inflation in an economy with a highly developed and complex capital structure would drastically falsify monetary calculation and cause capital consumption and a drastic plunge in living standards.

(3) Another area in which we face the prospect of calculational chaos is health care. By wildly subsidizing and stimulating the demand for health care services of selected special interest groups beginning in the mid-1960s, the United States government precipitated a never ending and catastrophic upward-spiral of health care costs.

In addition, the irrational and labyrinthine structure of regulations and prohibitions imposed by government on the industry has massively distorted resource allocation, restricted supply, and further driven up the costs of medical care. The tragic but predictable result of such intervention is that many of the unsubsidized members of society have been effectively priced out of the market for health care. The simple and humane solution to this tragedy is to quickly terminate these antisocial subsidies and dismantle the destructive regulatory structure, permitting the competitive price appraisement and resource allocation process to operate unimpeded.

But, of course, the internal dynamic of the welfare state is never to retrench and risk disaffection of its pampered and powerful constituencies, for example, the American Medical Association, the American Association for Retired Persons, the entrenched bureaucracies of nonprofit hospitals, and so on. And so we face the prospect of "national health care insurance" which is a euphemism for the thoroughgoing socialization of the health care sector, with its resultant shortages, further suppression of competitive incentives, and deterioration of quality. But this is simply another example of the mad logic of the welfare state: since the government produces nothing that is valuable in terms of social appraisement, it can only supply welfare to some by siphoning off the resources and destroying the economic arrangements that support the welfare of others. In attempting to repair the politically unpopular destruction of its earlier policies, it is driven to further isolated acts of destruction until it arrives, with cruel and ultimate irony, at the policy for the systematic destruction of society and human welfare, that is, socialism.

(4) Finally, we have environmental policies, which are becoming progressively broader in scope and more draconian in enforcement. To the extent that such policies go beyond the protection of individual rights and property—and they are now far, far beyond this point—they become antisocial and destructive of capital and living standards. In fact, in many if not in most cases, it is the obliteration of economic productivity *per se* which is intended and which constitutes the in-kind welfare subsidy to the well-heeled and well-organized minority of upper-middle class environmentalists.

This is true, for example, of environmental regulations that prohibit development activities for the vast majority of Alaskan land and along much of the California coastline as well as of recent calls for suppressing development of the Amazon rain forest and coercively maintaining the entire continent of Antarctica forever wild.

Needless to say, thoroughgoing and centralized land use regulations, which some fanatical environmentalists are calling for, is tantamount to the abolition of private property in natural resources and business structures. The connection between environmentalism and socialism is even stronger when we realize that what socialism brings about unintentionally—the abolition of humanity as a teleological force shaping nature to its purposes—is precisely the aim of the radical environmentalist program.

Conclusion

The significance of Mises's 1920 article extends far beyond its devastating demonstration of the impossibility of socialist economy and society. It provides the rationale for the price system, purely free markets, the security of private property against all encroachments, and sound money. Its thesis will continue to be relevant as long as economists and policy makers want to understand why even minor government economic interventions consistently fail to achieve socially beneficial results. "Economic Calculation in the Socialist Commonwealth" surely ranks among the most important economic articles written this century.

Joseph T. Salerno
Associate Professor of Economics
Lubin Graduate School of Business
Pace University
April 1990

About the author ...

Ludwig von Mises
(1881 - 1973)

The economist of the century. Throughout seven decades of teaching and writing, Ludwig von Mises reconstructed the whole of economics on a sound foundation of reason and human action. He was born in 1881 in the Austro-Hungarian city of Lemberg, the son of a successful engineer. At the age of 19, he entered the University of Vienna, and received his doctorate at 27. He studied in the stimulating tradition of Carl Menger and Eugen Böhm-Bawerk and eventually went on to surpass his teachers.

Mises published his first great work, *The Theory of Money and Credit*, in 1912 which made the 31-year old Mises one of the top economists in Europe. But with World War I driving economists and universities away from laissez-faire, Mises was never given the academic position that was his due. He taught at the University of Vienna, but as an unpaid *privatdozent*. So from 1909 to 1934, he was economic advisor to the Austrian Chamber of Commerce, during which time he established the Austrian Institute for Business Cycle Research and held a weekly private seminar attracting scholars from all over Europe.

Seeing that the Nazis were coming to power in Austria, Mises left to teach in Switzerland and then moved to the United States, where he eventually secured a non-paying visiting professorship at New York University, thanks to the help of economist and businessman Lawrence Fertig. Mises's lifetime of scholarly output resulted in 25 books and over 250 articles. Since his death in 1973, his writings have inspired a resurgence in free-market thought and a growing number of scholars who associate themselves with the Austrian school of economics.

Ludwig von Mises

Murray N. Rothbard

The Ludwig von Mises Institute

The Ludwig von Mises Institute, established in 1982 and named for the great anti-statist economist, advances the cause of liberty, free markets, sound money, and private property, on campus and in American life.

Founded on the counsel of Mrs. Ludwig von Mises, who served as chairman until her death, the Institute was also privileged to have famed economist Murray N. Rothbard as its academic vice president. Other eminent associates have included Nobelist F. A. Hayek and the great journalist Henry Hazlitt. Today, it has an international faculty of more than one hundred scholars working in the same tradition.

Supported entirely by private donations, the Institute publishes five periodicals, including an academic journal, *The Review of Austrian Economics*, three quarterlies, including *The Mises Review* and *The Austrian Economics Newsletter*, and a monthly, *The Free Market*, as well as books, monographs, study guides, op-eds, and occasional papers.

The Institute provides fellowships to Austrian School graduate students and sponsors a wide range of teaching programs, including the acclaimed summer Mises University, attracting students from all over the country and the world. The Institute also holds topical conferences on such subjects as war, bureaucracy, central banking, the gold standard, and secessionism.

Contributions to the Ludwig von Mises Institute are tax-deductible to the full extent of the law, and are welcomed from individuals, families, businesses, and foundations. To join the Institute, send a contribution of $25, $50, $100, or more. Student memberships are available at no charge (send a copy of your current student ID). For more information, write or call us, or visit our web page.

The Ludwig von Mises Institute
Auburn, Alabama 36849-5301
334-844-2500; fax: 334-844-2583
http://www.mises.org